EXTREME JUMPERS

BLACKBIRCH PRESS

An imprint of Thomson Gale, a part of The Thomson Corporation

THOMSON

GALE

Detroit • New York • San Francisco • San Diego • New Haven, Conn. • Waterville, Maine • London • Munich

THOMSON

✳

™

GALE

For more information, contact
Blackbirch Press
27500 Drake Rd.
Farmington Hills, MI 48331-3535
Or you can visit our Internet site at http://www.gale.com

Photo credits: cover: Photos.com, Corel Corporation, CORBIS; all pages © Discovery Communications, Inc. except for pages 4, 5, 39 © Corel Corporation; page 7 © Photodisc; page 9 © W.P. Armstrong; page 12 © Lonely Planet; page 16, 19, 20, 32 © Photos.com; page 24, 36, 37, 40 © CORBIS

LIBRARY OF CONGRESS CATALOGING-IN-PUBLICATION DATA

Jumpers / Marla Felkins Ryan, book editor
   p. cm. — (Planet's most extreme)

Includes bibliographical references and index.
  ISBN: 1-4103-0377-2 (hard cover : alk. paper)
    1-4103-0355-7 (paper cover : alk. paper)
  1. Animal behavior—Juvenile literature. 2. Risk-taking (Psychology) — Juvenile literature. I. Ryan, Marla Felkins, 1958- II. Title III. Series.

Printed in the United States of America
10 9 8 7 6 5 4 3 2 1

THE MOST EXTREME
Animal Planet

Some people love getting high—but how do they measure up to the best jumpers in the animal world? Find out as our top ten countdown of the most extreme jumpers on the planet takes us to surprising new heights.

10

The **Rabbit**

Leaping straight into the countdown at number ten are animals born to be jumpers. Rabbits and hares can't walk. They can't trot. They have to jump—all the time. They kick off the countdown because those big back legs are incredibly powerful.

At number ten, the rabbit uses its powerful back legs to kick off our countdown.

Watching a bunny hopping gently in a field, you'd never guess the extreme distance it can leap. You have to see it sprinting to discover how far it can jump in a single bound!

The rabbit's back legs are like coiled springs. They power the leaps that can carry the rabbit 10 times its body length. That's a jump of up to 19 feet!

With the amazing spring action of its back legs, the rabbit is one extreme jumper.

**A rabbit can leap a distance almost
10 times its body length in just one jump.**

Compare that to the distance Olympic athletes can jump. If you
could leap like a rabbit, you'd jump twice as far as any human
in history—an incredible 60 feet!

Our leg muscles are about the same strength as a rabbit's, so how
can rabbits jump so much farther than us? It all comes down to
body weight. The heavier you are, the harder it is for those muscles
to push you off the ground. That's why lightweight bunnies are
such extreme jumpers.

Which bunny is the best of the best? To find out, these people are attending a most unusual race meeting. Competitors have traveled here from all around Sweden and are highly trained athletes. These pampered pets are here to compete in the *kaninhop*—the Scandinavian sport of rabbit jumping.

Recently, rabbit jumping arrived in the United States. American bunnies may have a little catching up to do to their Scandinavian counterparts. And while these domesticated rabbits may have lost a little of the agility of their wild ancestors, the sport is actually all about fun, according to the president of the Rabbit Hopping Organization of America, Linda Hoover:

> *I think rabbits learn that this is going to be a fun sport. The kids get excited. It goes right down the lead and the bunnies get very excited by it. Everyone who sees a hopping event goes out and gets their bunny and tries it, so I think it's going to evolve into a great sport throughout the United States.*

American bunnies have recently gotten in on the sport of rabbit jumping.

Maybe one day with a lot of practice, one of these rabbits could put our Olympic athletes to shame.

7

9

The Mexican
Jumping Bean

Our next contender could never compete in the Animal Olympics, for the simple reason that it isn't an animal! Or is it?

Mexican jumping beans are number nine in our countdown, but how does a bean jump?

To find this contender, biologists Dave Riherd and Paul Hahn have hopped down to Little Mexico in Los Angeles. For hiding somewhere in these market stalls is the most unusual animal in the countdown.

Our number nine is truly extreme because these guys first have to find a plant. Well, a bean actually. But these are no ordinary beans. These are Mexican jumping beans.

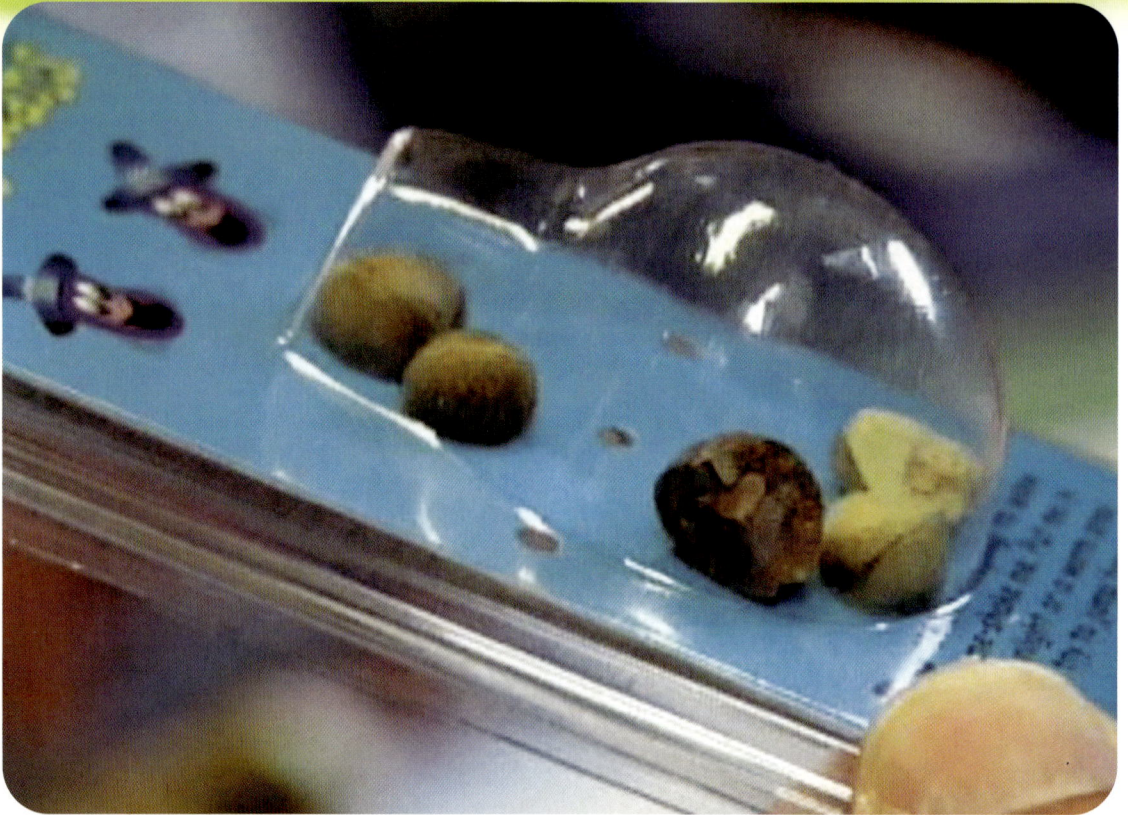

These beans have a secret inside them. They're home to tiny residents.

Some people think jumping beans are just a joke—a novelty you only see in old comedies—but Mexican jumping beans really jump! For these beans, jumping is no joke. It's a matter of survival. How do they do it? What makes a bean jump?

To find out, you need to take a look inside at the most unusual jumping device in the world. It's a caterpillar. These are larvae of little bugs, and what they do is crawl around inside the fruit and they eat it, and that sustains them until the springtime, when they hatch out.

It's this caterpillar that makes the bean jump, because it hates getting hot. It'll throw itself around inside the shell to get the bean on the move. The Mexican jumping caterpillar is just trying to get its house back in the shade.

For a bug in a bean, this is a pretty extreme jumping ability. But our countdown of the most extreme jumping animals on the planet is just warming up.

This caterpillar throws its weight around to get where it wants to go.

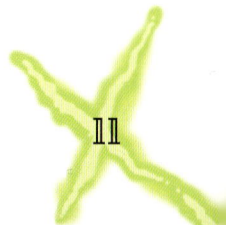

8

The Bharal

How'd you like to live on the highest mountains in the world? It's a land of ice and precipice. And it's home sweet home for the Tibetan bharal, a mountain sheep that lives life on the edge.

The Tibetan bharal lives on the highest mountains in the world.

Bharal are number eight in our countdown because they're extraordinary rock hoppers. They have to be. When you live above 14,000 feet in these mountains, one slip can be fatal.

Male bharals are extremely confident in their jumping ability. In fact, they show off by trying to knock each other off the cliff!

Bharal may be happy bouncing off rocks, but most humans try to hang on for dear life. We use ropes, crampons—anything to get a grip on the cliff.

13

Not bharals, though. All their climbing equipment is packed into their feet. Those hooves are rubbery to increase their gripping potential. And they're flexible. Bharals can spread their toes out to grasp the ground, and to have some brakes when sliding down an icy slope!

Since human mountaineers can't tiptoe down the rocks like bharals, they've had to come up with a different way of getting down the mountain. It's a little extreme, but a lot faster.

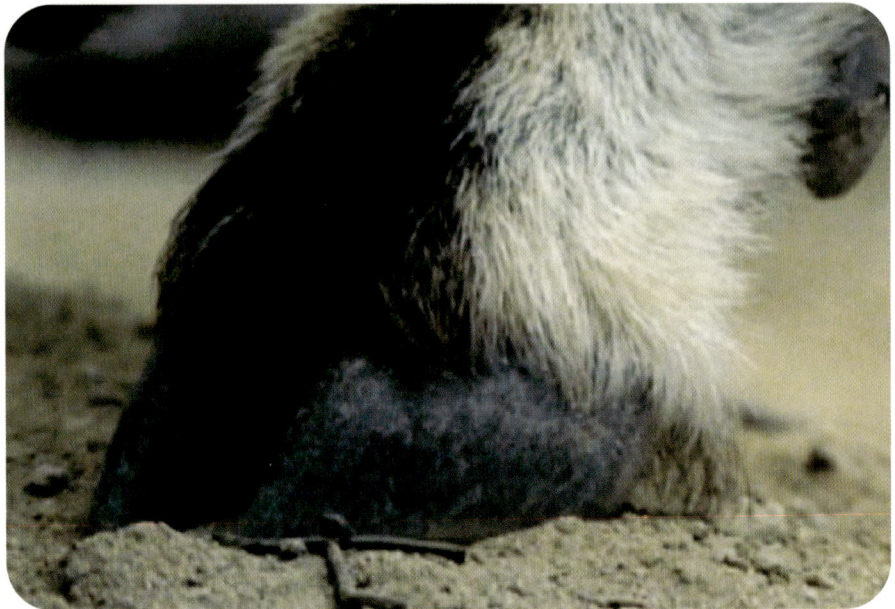

Rubbery hooves help the bharal grip even the most slippery slope.

Even bharal kids are extreme jumpers. Look at that one go!

This is the extreme sport of base jumping. You find a cliff, and you jump off. Kids—don't try this at home.

Of course, this is home for bharal kids, and these kids don't have a parachute if they fall. These impossibly high cliffs are a dangerous place to grow up. In fact, only half the kids born each year will celebrate their first birthday.

Those sure-footed babies that survive really are extreme jumpers. In fact, sometimes they seem to take as much pleasure in leaping down the mountain as any adrenaline junkie with a parachute!

The **Locust**

Number seven in our extreme countdown may be small, but what it lacks in size, it makes up for in sheer numbers. These are locusts. It's a good old-fashioned biblical plague of horrible hoppers. Locusts are a kind of grasshopper, and they can really hop over a lot of grass. A locust's huge hind legs can kick it more than 3 feet—or 20 times its body length!

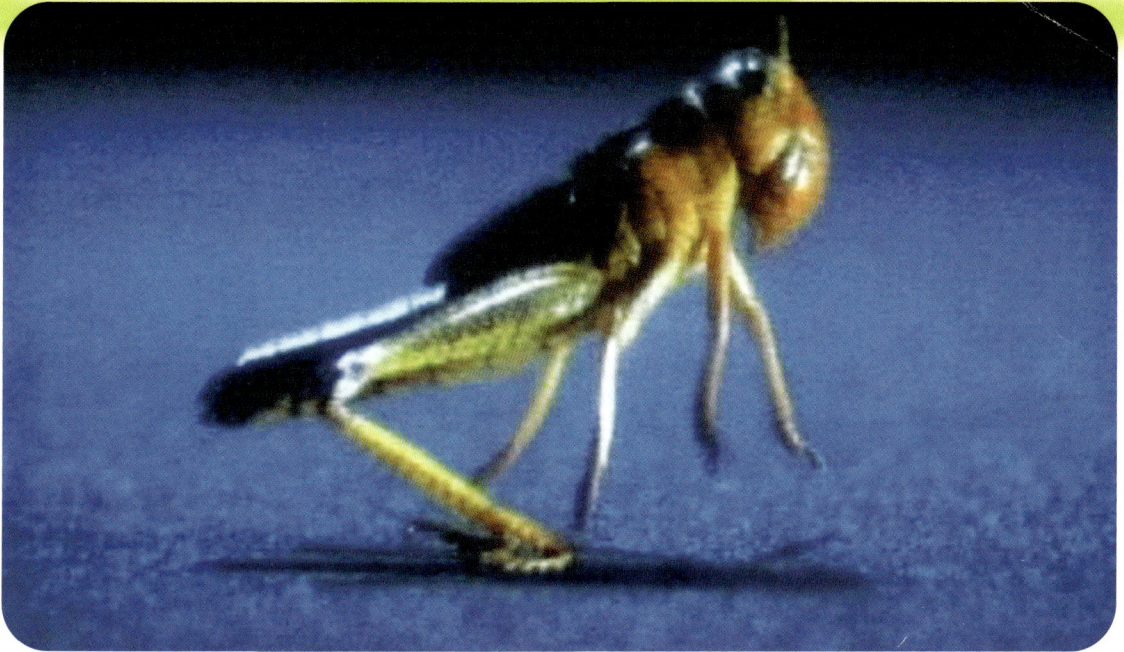

Elastic bands in the locust's knees help it leap to number seven.

Imagine if a basketball player could jump like a locust. How would you like to be able to jump 300 feet for the ultimate slam-dunk?

Basketball players would love to have legs like a locust. That's because in addition to the massive muscles in its thighs, the locust has elastic bands in its knees. These bands are like stretchy springs that store energy. They work a bit like our tendons, which store enough energy to let us snap our fingers.

When you push your thumb against your finger, the tendons of the muscles are stretching, storing more and more energy until . . . snap! That rapid finger movement has mostly been powered from energy stored in the springy tendons. And that's how the locust's springy knees power those magnificent jumps.

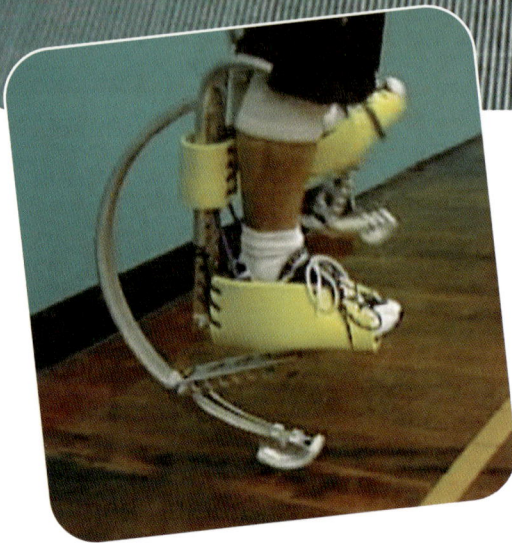

The Powerskipper can make you jump like a grasshopper because its flexible bands work just like a locust's knee.

Soon it may be possible for anyone to put a little extra spring in their stride. Even the shortest basketball players could slam dunk with the best of them, with a little help of an artificial knee.

The flexible bands of the Powerskipper store energy like the locust's knee. And when the energy is released, you get a jump that would make any grasshopper proud.

Grasshoppers may be great jumpers, but they can have trouble in the romance department. When you're in long grass it can be hard to see a prospective partner—no matter how high you hop. That's why grasshoppers have another string to their bow legs.

Males make music with those bulging thighs. They advertise how strong they are by rubbing those long jumping legs against their body. Their inner thighs are lined with a row of pegs that lets them scrape out their high-pitched love song. And the better the music, the more successful the male.

Male locusts rub their legs against their bodies to make beautiful music that's a hit with the ladies.

X6

The **Kangaroo**

While the next animal in the countdown may not be able to hold a tune, it too can do amazing things with its legs. At number six is an animal the Western world only discovered when European explorers first arrived in Australia.

According to legend, when they first set foot on this new land they saw a strange animal hopping about. So they asked a local aboriginal what it was called. The aboriginal said: "kangaroo."

Unfortunately, in aboriginal "kangaroo" doesn't mean "large jumping animal," but translates as "I don't understand your question." So Australia is now home to more than sixty species of "I don't understand your questions."

No matter what they're called, though, kangaroos are extreme athletes. It's not just the fact that they're incredible jumpers. They're also extremely fast!

A kangaroo would rather jump than walk any day.

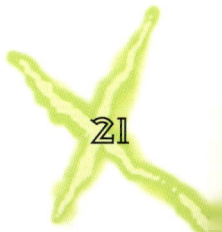

A sprinting kangaroo would clean up at the Olympics. It travels twice the speed of the world's fastest sprinters! That means it would win the Olympic 100-meter sprint in a time of 4 seconds! And then over in the long-jump pit, every 30-foot bounce would win an Olympic gold medal! But the really amazing thing about these extreme athletes is that the faster a kangaroo travels, the less energy it uses!

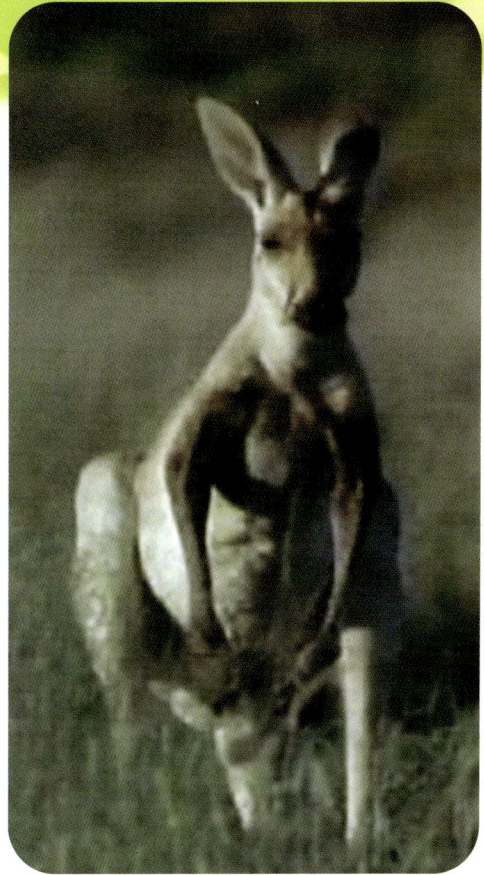

When we want to run faster, we have to increase the number of strides we take each second. All this extra effort means we burn much more energy sprinting than walking. But kangaroos are different.

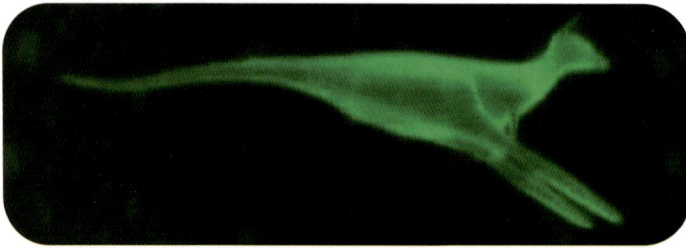

The kangaroo's body is built to store jumping energy.

To go faster, a kangaroo doesn't take more steps. It simply increases the length of its jump. And the farther the kangaroo jumps, the more energy it's able to store in the massive tendons of its legs and tail. In fact, a kangaroo is so good at storing jumping energy that it's actually easier for it to run than to walk.

Some people have made use of a different method of storing energy for a high jump. In the frozen lands of the Arctic, hunters had a problem. The sea ice was so flat that it was really hard to get high enough to be able to see things in the distance. Their solution was to get fifty friends and a really big blanket!

The blanket toss is now a favorite event in the Eskimo-Indian Olympics. Judges award points according to grace, height, and smoothness of landing! But once, this wasn't just a sport. It was an old hunting technique to give the added elevation needed to spot prey far across the sea ice.

Kangaroos can jump 30 feet in a single bounce.

We use a similar jumping device today—but not to spot whales. And instead of a blanket we use an invention that was inspired by a very different kind of festival.

In Iowa back in 1930, 11-year-old George Nissen loved watching circus trapeze artists bounce into the safety nets. It started him thinking. Over the next few years he developed the idea of stretching canvas between springs. But he still didn't know what to call his invention until he traveled to Mexico. He loved the sound of the Spanish word for diving board, and that's how we got El Trampolin! Unfortunately, no amount of canvas and springs can match the power in the amazing legs of the kangaroo.

5

The **Kangaroo Rat**

We're halfway through the countdown, and our search for the fifth most extreme jumping animal on the planet has taken us to the heart of Mongolia and the Gobi desert. The kangaroos of Australia are half a world away. Or are they?

The kangaroo rat uses its back legs just like a kangaroo does and can clear 15 feet with just one jump.

This is a kangaroo. Actually it's a kangaroo rat—a rodent that uses those long back legs just like a kangaroo does. But the kangaroo rat takes hopping to new extremes, because a single bound can carry it 15 feet. That's an incredible 45 times its body length!

Imagine if a tall football player could jump that far. It would be hard to defend against a player that could leap from end zone to end zone!

Such extreme jumping hasn't gone unnoticed. In fact, these desert athletes once caught the eye of an army. In World War II, a division of the British army was proud to be called the desert rats.

The nickname came from German propaganda that called the soldiers "rats" hiding in holes in the desert. It didn't take long for the division to adopt the kangaroo rat as its mascot.

These rodents burrow into holes to survive their harsh desert habitat.

The desert rat was even a mascot for British soldiers during World War II!

As the Desert Rats continued fighting, they took with them their mascot—the kangaroo rat—painted on the sides of their vehicles.

4

The **Klipspringer**

The kangaroo rat may have been popular with the troops in World War II, but coming in at number four in the countdown is an animal that would be a star on any stage in the world.

Ballet dancers are the most graceful professional jumpers in the world. They train for years to stand on the very tips of their toes. But our next animal in the countdown has been jumping on tiptoe for millions of years.

This is a klipspringer—the "balle-rina of the rocks." This dainty little antelope lives high on rocky outcrops that jut up from the plains of Africa. Early Dutch settlers named these animals "klipspringer." It means "rock jumper," and it's easy to see how they got their name.

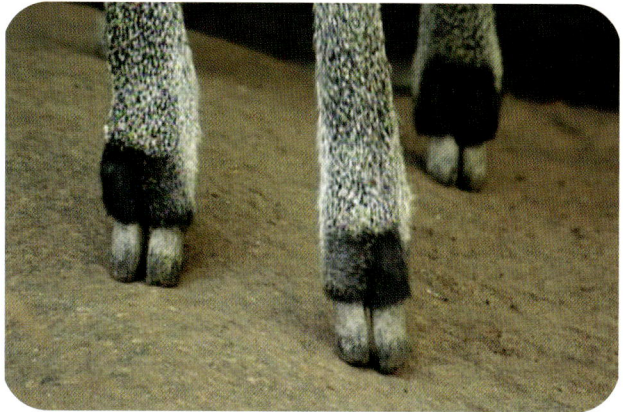

Klipspringers stand, walk, and jump on tiptoe.

Like any ballerina, the klipspringer dances lightly on the tips of its amazing toes. Its extreme jumping ability is also useful to keep out of the clutches of Honolulu zookeeper Greg Hamilton. He explains:

> In the middle of this split hoof is a fleshy area that basically allows them to grip fairly readily to rock surfaces and allows them to maintain their positions on the rock. Their ability to escape is to get into areas that are inaccessible to other animals. These guys can land on a shelf that is about the size of a quarter and stay there.

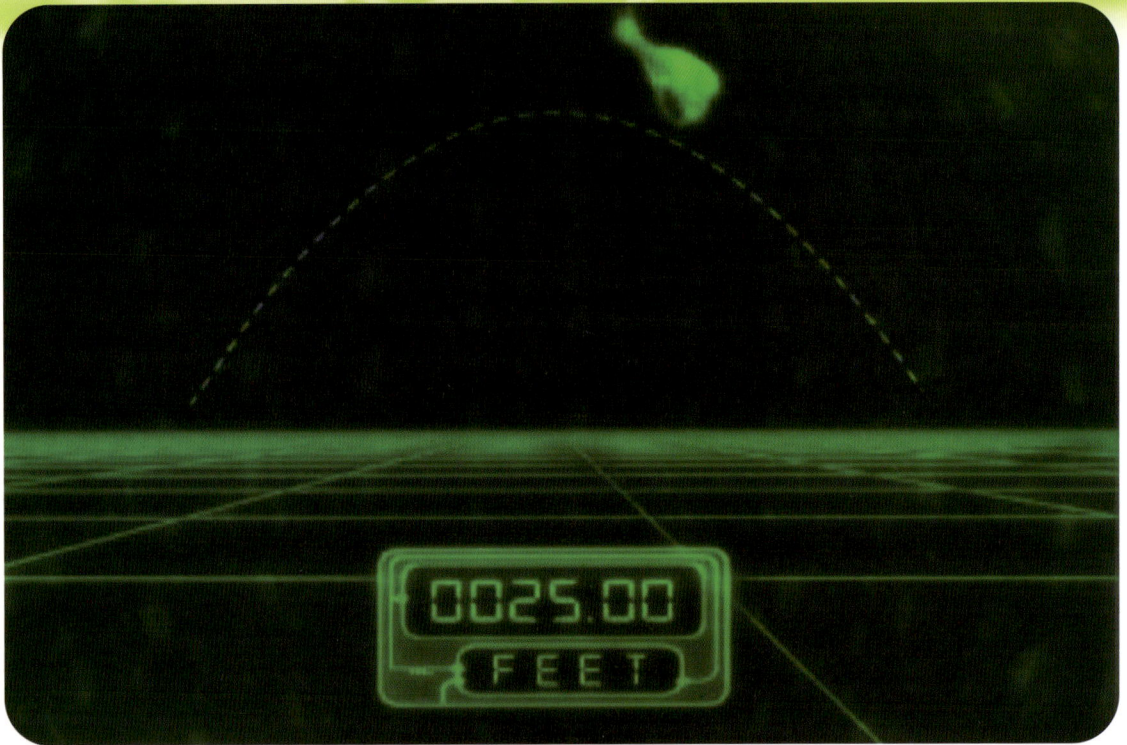

These graceful antelopes can jump 25 feet in the air.

What makes these rock hoppers different from other mountain goats is their extreme leaping. The klipspringer may be tiny, but it can leap 15 times it's own height! That's 25 feet! The best Olympic high jumpers can't clear even twice their height! But if they could jump like a klipspringer, they could leap from the shoulder of the Statue of Liberty and soar more 75 feet right over the torch! It's no wonder that looking after such extreme leapers can be a bit of a challenge. Greg Hamilton explains:

One day I came in here and spooked the male Zulu and he started doing laps around the exhibit. Came through this area, bounced off this rock right here, and was about at least 3 feet above my head. And I'm six three so that was at least 9 feet in the air and he sailed with perfect ease. It was really amazing to watch him jump to that height.

We could never rock hop like a klipspringer, but there is one invention that sure makes it fun to try—the pogo stick. According to legend, there was once a poor farmer in the country formerly known as Burma. The farmer invented the prototype jumping stick to help his daughter dodge muddy puddles on the path to a temple. And the name of the farmer's daughter? Pogo—of course.

Even though klipspringers have four built-in pogo sticks, they're still only number four in our Most Extreme countdown. It seems incredible that anything could leap ahead of klipspringers, desert rats, or kangaroos. But coming in at number three in our countdown is an animal that can jump so far, it's frightening.

He may be tiny, but the klipspringer is a true extreme jumper.

3 The Jumping Spider

If you're afraid of spiders, just wait till you see what these guys can do. Leaping in at number three in the countdown are the jumping spiders. These guys are the lions of the spider world. They have exceptional eyesight, which means they can spot their lunch from a long way off. Then, like a big cat, they'll slowly sneak up on their prey and pounce. And what a pounce it can be!

The jumping spider can jump so far it looks like its flying!

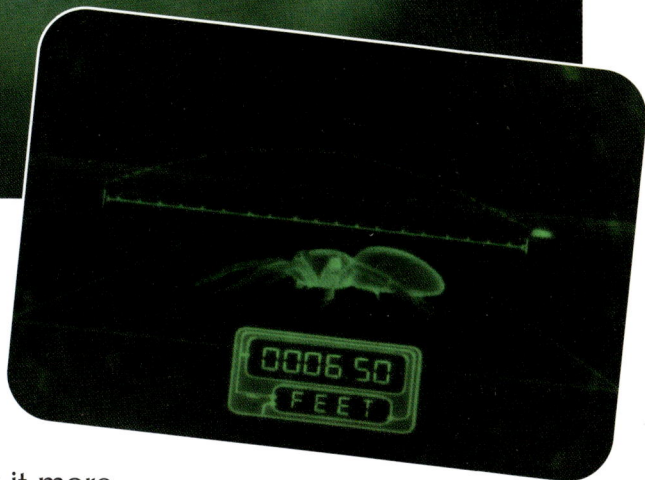

The jumping spider can really jump. Those eight legs can push it more than 6 feet—that's 100 times its body length!

A human athlete who could jump 100 times his body length might as well be flying! It would be like leaping clear over two jumbo jets, well over 400 feet!

You'd think that to jump such enormous distances, the spider's legs would be amazing—that they'd have to have bulging thighs packed with muscles. That's what human jumpers need. That's because human jumpers need well developed thighs and firm bottoms to get their bodies up into the air, and to absorb the shock of the landing.

But you don't need a firm bottom to look for jumping spiders. You just need good eyesight. Luckily, Canterbury Museum spider expert Simon Pollard has a good set of glasses and an excellent understanding of how spiders and humans move. He explains:

A spider like this has no trouble catching a dragonfly.

The way that we use our muscles is that we tend to have two pairs. We have muscles that do this and muscles that do that. But in the case of spiders, they have muscles that do this but rely on fluid under pressure to push the muscles out and the leg out. So when it comes to jumping, what these spiders do is increase the pressure of the fluid in the back legs, making them go straight. And because the spider's so small, it can jump from A to B and can do it very, very well. Going from one leaf to another to catch prey is of course what spiders do—they catch things. And a lot of what they catch can fly away. So being able to jump across this space is effectively like flying, and they can catch a flying insect.

The best part about being a jumping spider is that it doesn't matter if you miss your landing zone. These guys spin their own safety harness out of silk.

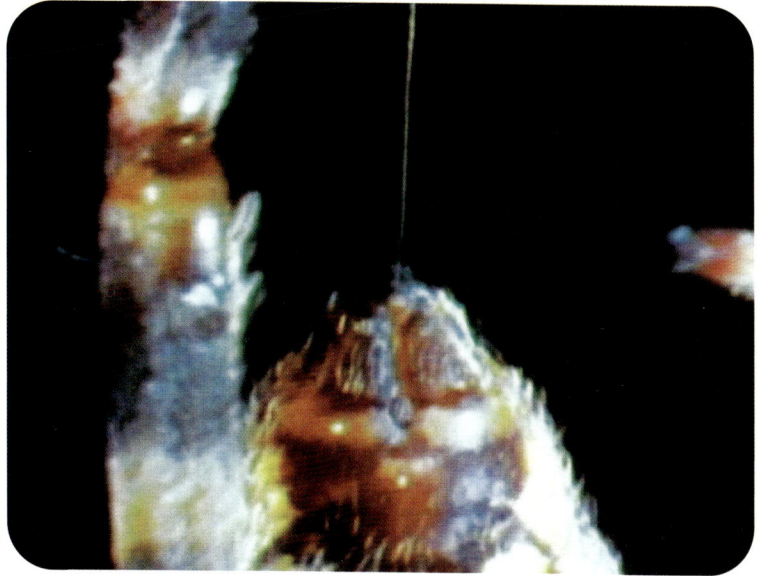

It can even spin its own safety harness.

But it's not just spiders that use a safety line when making death-defying leaps! On the Pacific Islands of Vanuatu, young men have been making huge leaps of faith. These guys don't use silk safety lines. They leap with nothing but two slim tree vines tied around their ankles!

The land divers of Vanuatu jump as part of the celebrations associated with the traditional festival of the yam harvest. It's a celebration that's caught on elsewhere—but not using tree vines.

Bungee jumping uses a latex rubber cord instead of tree vines, or spider silk. But the advantage spiders have over bungee jumpers is that once they've made their death-defying leap—they can eat their silk safety line!

2 The Jumping Frog

Safety lines are not enough for our next contender in the countdown. There's one animal that jumps so high it needs a parachute!

At number two in our countdown, frogs are the most legendary jumpers of all.

Frogs are legendary jumpers. Anyone who's taken a good look at a frog knows that its leaping ability lies in its long, long legs. When scientists compared the power available in the frog's leg muscles to the

Those long legs are made for extreme jumping.

distance they jumped, they discovered a frog can leap up to 7 times farther than was thought physically possible!

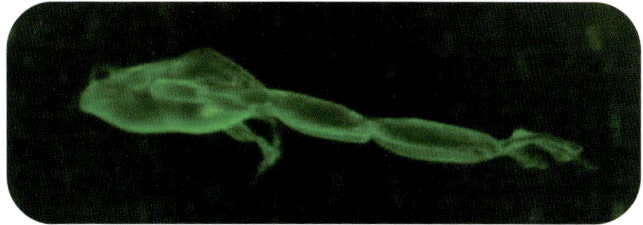

So the scientists took a closer look at the frog's legs. They discovered a trigger mechanism that allows the muscles to stretch the tendons, store the energy, and release it in that explosive leap!

There's serious competition at the Frog Jumping Jubilee in Calaveras County, California.

The question is, just how far can a frog jump? People have been trying to find out at the annual Frog Jumping Jubilee in Calaveras County, California. For more than 70 years, frog jockeys of all ages have been encouraging their frogs to triple jump their way to glory!

The winner of the Frog Jumping Jubilee may triple jump more than 20 feet, but that's not even half the distance covered by the most extreme jumping frog in the world.

Some tree frogs can jump a record 50 feet between trees!

High in the forests of Southeast Asia lives a tree frog with a difference. It's a frog with extra webbing between its toes. And so when it leaps out of a tree it opens four little parachutes.

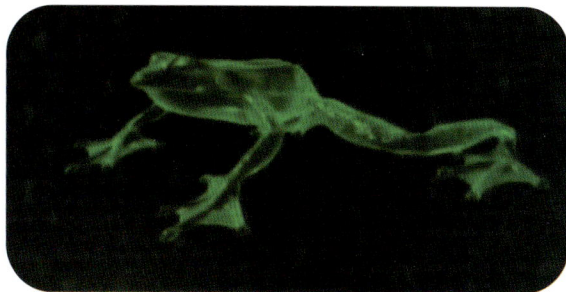

The webbing between its toes allows it to glide through the air.

These flying frogs can glide more than 50 feet between trees. Imagine being able to jump 150 times your body length. You'd be able to leap clear over the SS *Titanic*— a distance of nearly 900 feet! Then you really would be "King of the World!" But the incredible frog is still only number two in our Most Extreme countdown.

1

The **Flea**

You don't have to travel far to find the Most Extreme jumper on the planet. In fact, it's often too close for comfort.

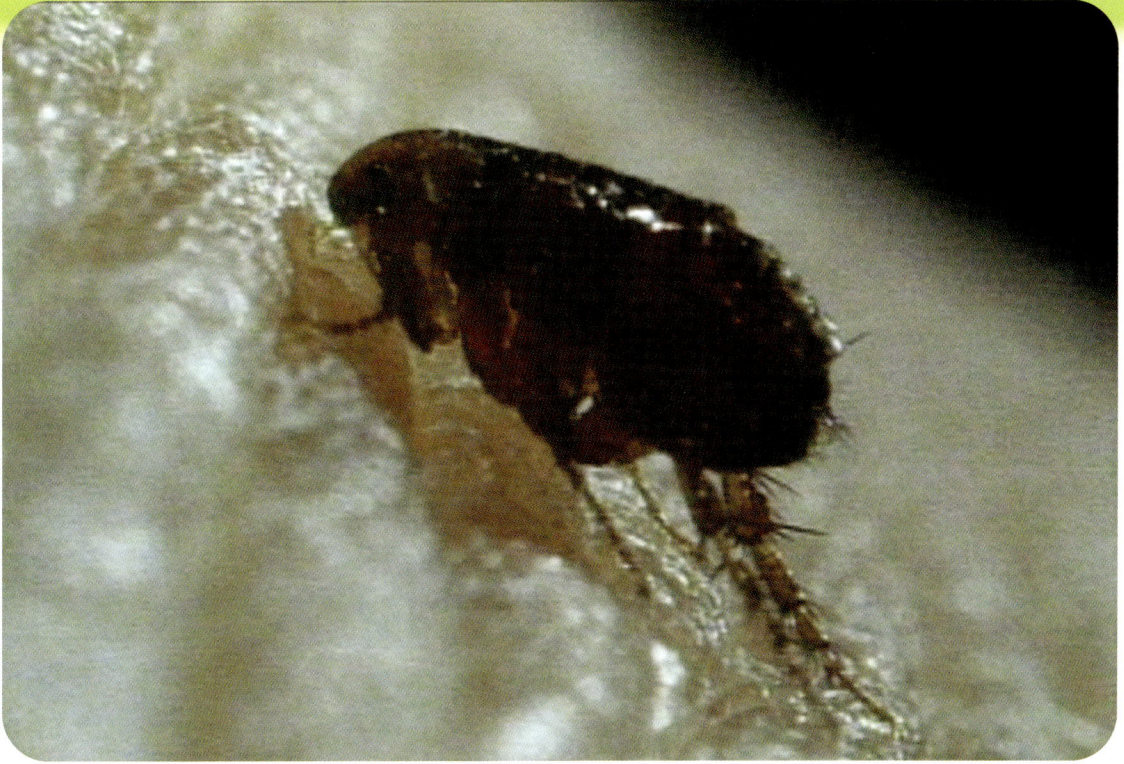

The most extreme jumper in the world isn't rare or exotic. It's the common flea.

It can spend months waiting patiently for entomologists like Ruud Kleinpaste to return home from vacation. Vibrations on the floorboards signal the time to leap into action.

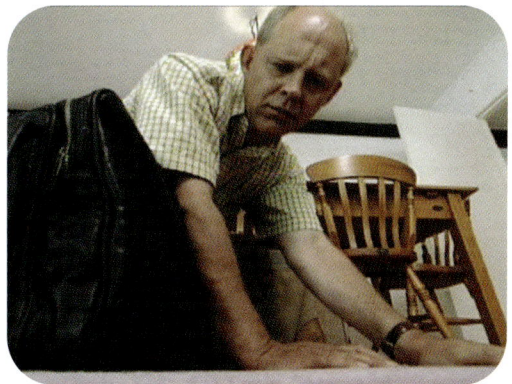

Too bad they're so hard to see.

The most extreme jumper in the world is the flea. A leap of 13 inches may be one small jump for a bug, but it's one giant leap for mankind. We're talking a leap that's 220 times your body length!

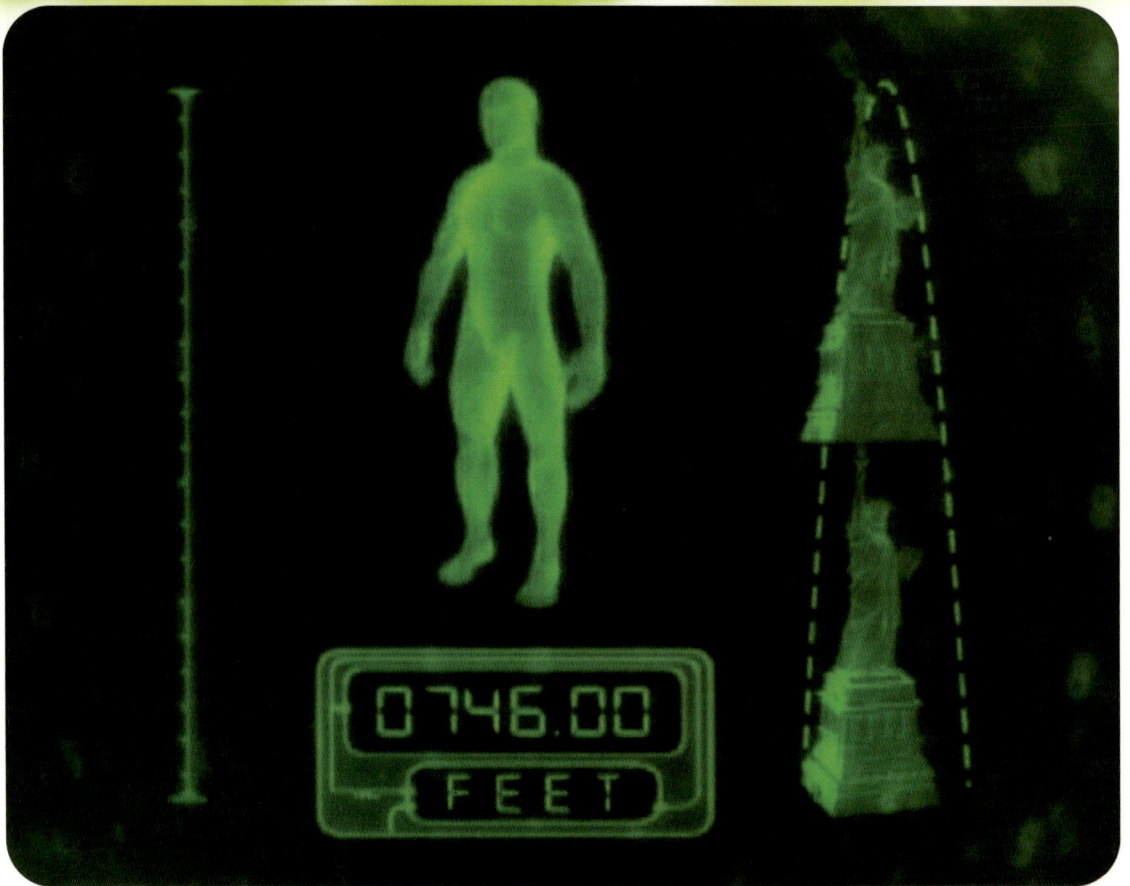

A human with the jumping power of a flea could jump over two Statues of Liberty.

With the super powers of a flea, we'd be able to clear the Brooklyn Bridge! That's nearly a quarter of a mile! But a flea can also jump more than 150 times its own height! That's like jumping over, not one, but two Statues of Liberty—more than 700 feet!

What makes fleas such extreme jumpers? They don't use muscle power like we do. Their legs work more like

42

a catapult. The flea stores muscle energy in a pad of resilin—which is one of the most elastic materials on the planet. It winds up this pad like a catapult, and then releases the trigger and POW! It releases all that energy at once and the flea jumps away.

Now that's an extreme jumper!

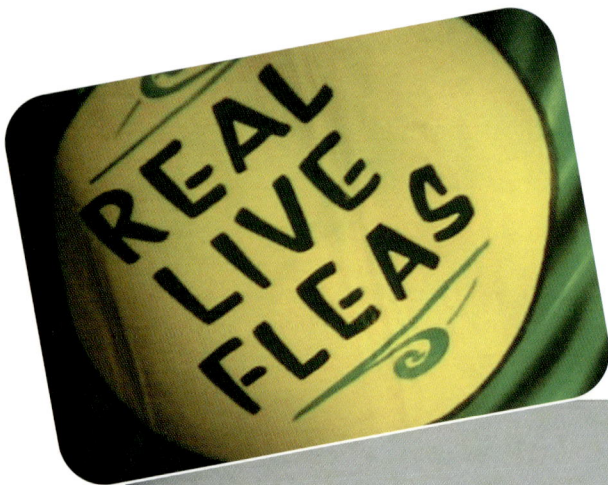

With such incredible powers, it's no wonder that people are prepared to pay to see performing fleas. Roll up, roll up to Maria Cardosa's Travelling Flea Circus. And here are the stars. Three hundred highly trained fleas.

The stars of Maria Cardosa's Travelling Flea Circus are highly trained.

These petite performers can even dance the tango. How's that for extreme?

Training begins by looping a tiny wire around the body, for no fleas are harmed for this performance. Once harnessed, the fleas are natural performers. They can be trained to follow the carbon dioxide breath of their trainers, jump towards the heat of a lamp, and even sway to the vibrations of the tango. It's lucky that fleas are used to traveling at enormous speeds. And like performers the world over, at the end of the show the fleas like to kick back, put their feet up, and have something to drink.

Love them or hate them, you just can't help being impressed by fleas. That's because when it comes to jumping, the flea really is . . . The Most Extreme.

For More Information

Jason Glaser, *Bungee Jumping.* Mankato, MN: Capstone, 2000.

Mary Ann McDonald, *Grasshoppers.* Chanhassen, MN: Child's World, 1998.

Alice B. McGinty, *Jumping Spider.* New York: Rosen, 2003.

Julie Murray, *Frogs.* Edina, MN: ABDO, 2004.

Julie Murray, *Jumping Spiders.* Edina, MN: ABDO, 2004.

Elaine Pascoe, *Crickets and Grasshoppers.* San Diego: Blackbirch, 1998.

Malcolm Penny, *Kangaroo.* Chicago: Raintree, 2004.

Richard Spilsbury, *Mob of Kangaroos.* Chicago: Heinemann, 2004.

Tanya Lee Stone, *Kangaroos.* San Diego: Blackbirch, 1998.

Samuel G. Woods, *Pogo Sticks.* San Diego: Blackbirch, 2001.

Glossary

aboriginal: member of the original native group to inhabit Australia

adrenaline: a hormone that helps the body deal with stress

catapult: a weapon used to hurl missiles

crampon: a framework of spikes attached to the bottom of a shoe to prevent slipping

domesticated: adapted to live closely with humans

entomologist: scientist who studies insects

larvae: the first stage of an insect after it hatches from an egg

plague: destructive outbreak

propaganda: communications intended to influence opinion

resilin: elastic protein substance

tendon: fibrous tissue that connects bones to other bodily structures

Index